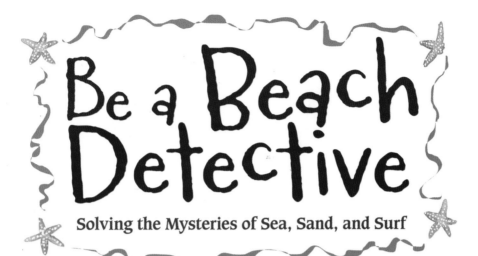

Be a Beach Detective

Solving the Mysteries of Sea, Sand, and Surf

Peggy Kochanoff

NIMBUS
PUBLISHING

Nimbus Publishing Limited
3731 Mackintosh St, Halifax, NS B3K 5A5
(902) 455-4286 nimbus.ca

Printed and bound in China

NB1140

Design: Jenn Embree

Library and Archives Canada Cataloguing in Publication

Kochanoff, Peggy, 1943-, author
Be a beach detective : solving the mysteries of sea, sand, and surf / Peggy Kochanoff.
Includes bibliographical references.
ISBN 978-1-77108-267-9 (pbk.)

1. Seashore biology—Juvenile literature. 2. Seashore—Juvenile literature. I. Title.

QH95.7.K53 2015   j578.769'9   C2014-907793-9

Nimbus Publishing acknowledges the financial support for its publishing activities from the Government of Canada through the Canada Book Fund (CBF) and the Canada Council for the Arts, and from the Province of Nova Scotia through Film & Creative Industries Nova Scotia. We are pleased to work in partnership with Film & Creative Industries Nova Scotia to develop and promote our creative industries for the benefit of all Nova Scotians.

Dedicated to my wonderful family (Stan, Tom, Jim, Avai, and Jaya) for all their support.

Thanks to Jim Wolford (retired biology teacher at Acadia University) for checking my nature facts and spelling.

Two-thirds of the earth is covered with water. Where water meets land, huge numbers of beaches form. Most of us have fond memories of summers spent exploring a beach and finding exciting shells and creatures. I hope this book helps explain what some of those are so you can enjoy your treasures even more. Please put live things back where you found them. Cherish and respect the environment.

Mermaid's Purse

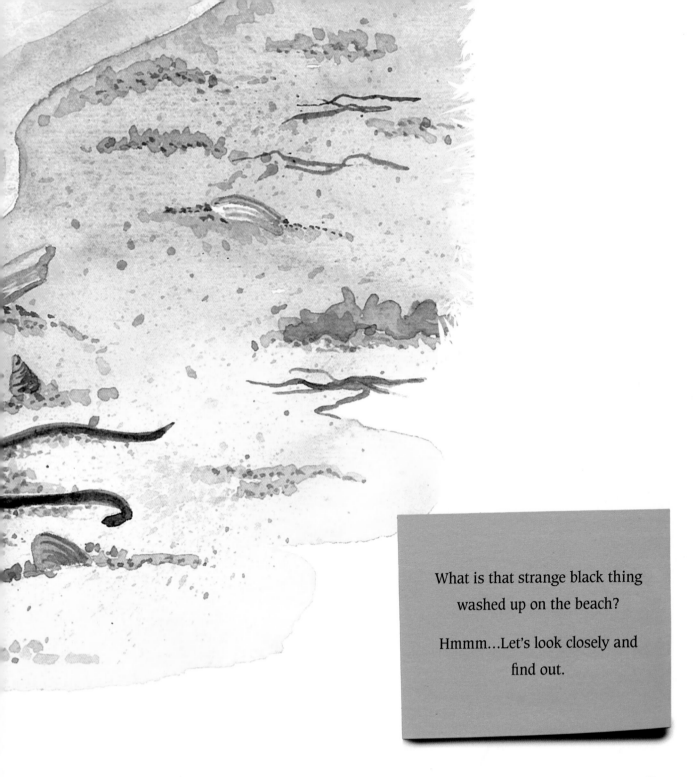

What is that strange black thing washed up on the beach?

Hmmm...Let's look closely and find out.

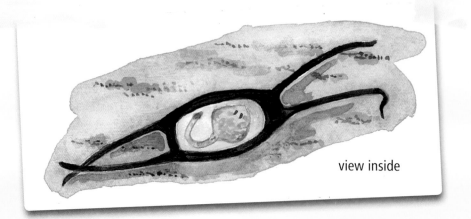

view inside

It is called a "mermaid's purse" and is actually an egg case that surrounds and protects the fertilized eggs of skates and some sharks. They are deposited on sandy or muddy bottoms in shallow water. Tendrils at each corner anchor the case to rocks, grass, or wood. Once laid, a sticky mesh of threads trap sand, which acts as an anchor. After the young hatch, the case is empty and lightweight and easily washed ashore.

Skates have enlarged fins at each side of their body that look like wings. The head, body, and fins are flat. Both eyes are on top so they can watch for attackers above. The mouth is on the bottom so they can swim close to the ocean floor searching for shellfish, fish, and **crustaceans**.

Mystery solved!

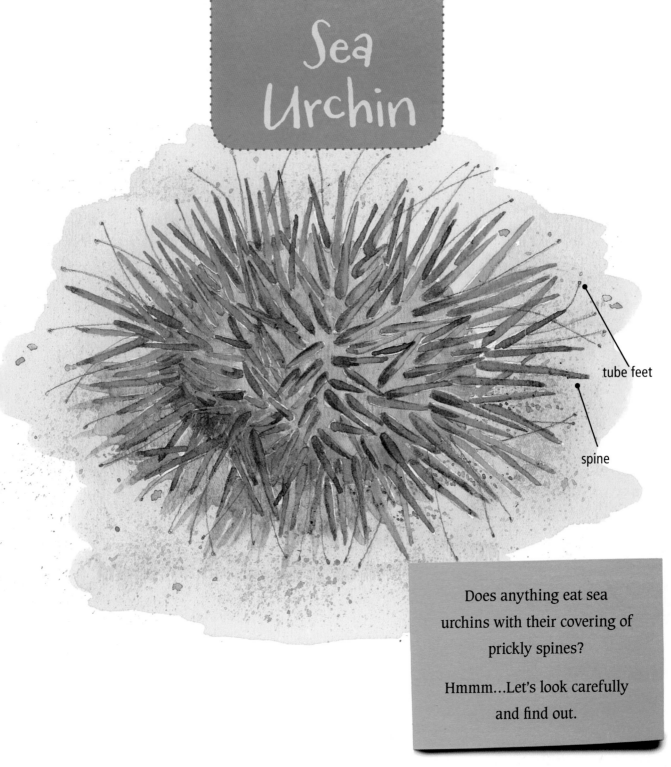

Sea Urchin

tube feet

spine

Does anything eat sea urchins with their covering of prickly spines?

Hmmm...Let's look carefully and find out.

Amazingly, urchins are eaten by some fish (cod, haddock, sculpin) as well as starfish, lobsters, some seabirds, and Pacific sea otters.

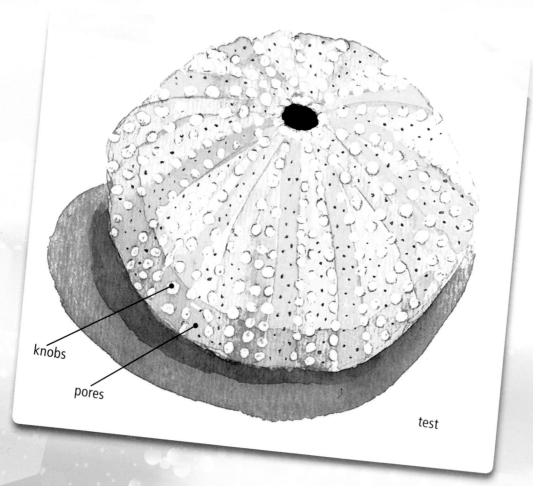

knobs

pores

test

Spines are used for locomotion and protection. Each spine moves on a ball-and-socket joint. **Tube feet** stick out beyond the spines through small pores. Different tube feet are used for breathing, locomotion, passing food to the mouth, and for anchoring the urchin to rocks and seaweed. When the urchin dies, spines fall off and a lumpy skeleton (called a test) is left. The spines moved on the knobs you see. Tiny pores are where the tube feet extended.

bottom view showing teeth

The mouth is on the bottom and contains five strong teeth that grow for the urchin's whole life. The teeth open and close like a beak and scrape algae for food. The teeth plus supporting muscles and cartilage are known as Aristotle's lantern.

Mystery solved!

Barnacle

How do barnacles survive when the tide goes out, leaving them exposed and dry?

Hmmm...Let's look closely and find out.

Larvae (half millimeter long) escape from eggs inside the barnacle and drift in the ocean.

Swimming larvae grow and change shape and find a mature colony. They turn upside down, and sucker-like tips of their antennae attach to boats, rocks, wood, shells, whales, crabs, etc.

Glue of amazing strength is squeezed from their head and cements the barnacle in place for life. Six rigid plates are secreted like the shape of a volcano. On top another two pairs of movable plates open and close for feeding and reproducing. When the tide goes out, the movable plates close tightly, protecting against the sun and drying air. With a little water trapped inside, the barnacle is kept alive until the tide comes back.

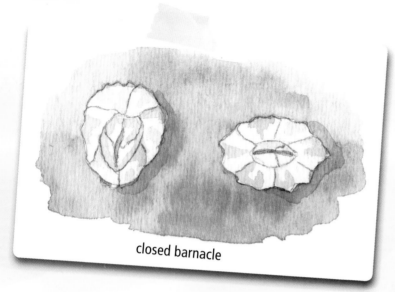

closed barnacle

open

Six pairs of hairy legs are now on top and sweep microscopic plants and animals found in the water into the barnacle's mouth. Cilia plus mucus help filter-feed.

Mystery solved!

Clam

Why does water squirt up as you walk along the beach?

Hmmm…Let's look closely and find out.

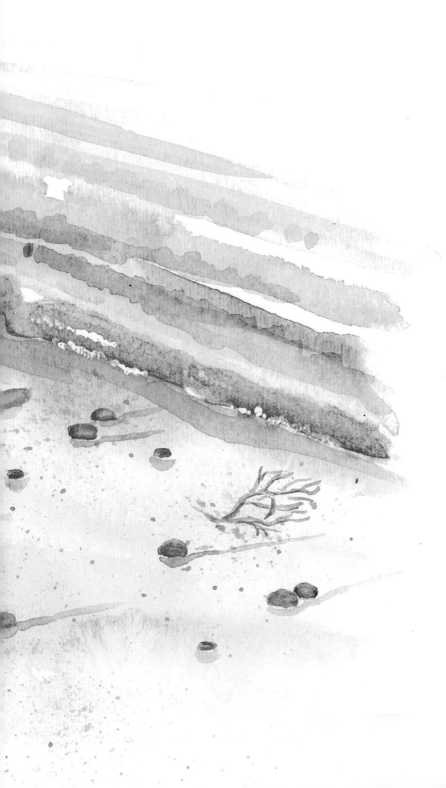

Living under the wet sand or mud are clams. They have tubes (**siphons**) that suck in water that is filtered in their gills for food and oxygen. Another siphon sends the used water out. When clams feel the vibration of your feet, they pull these tubes inside their shells. This causes any water in the siphons to squirt out. Then they close their two shell parts and retreat more deeply to escape into the sand.

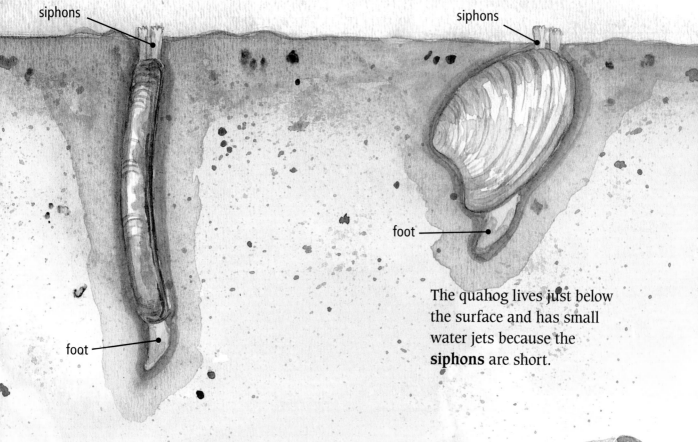

razor clam

siphons

quahog

siphons

foot

foot

The quahog lives just below the surface and has small water jets because the **siphons** are short.

Because of its streamlined shape and strong muscular foot, a razor clam digs into the sand with amazing speed and is very hard to catch. When its two short **siphons** are pulled in, a small water jet shoots up. The narrow shell is six to seven inches long and lives in a vertical position. Its name comes from the resemblance to an old-fashioned razor.

Dark purple inside the thick shell was used by Aboriginal peoples to make beads and as money

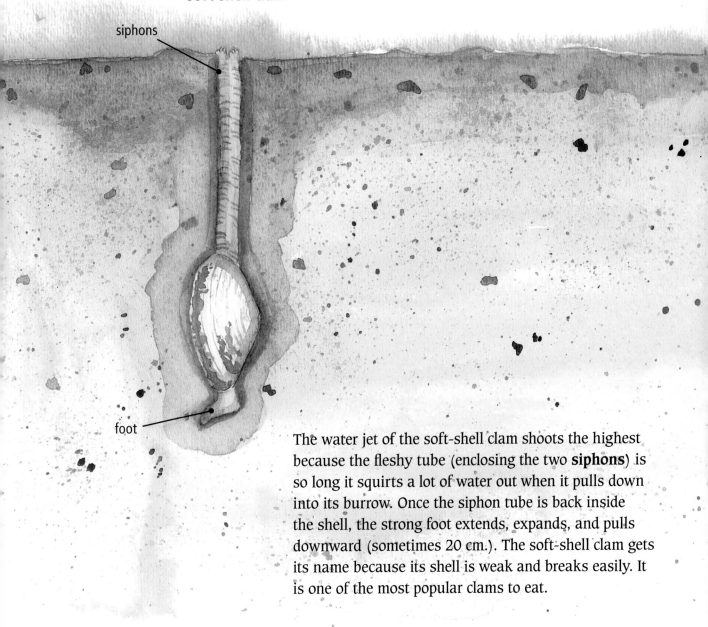

soft-shell clam

siphons

foot

The water jet of the soft-shell clam shoots the highest because the fleshy tube (enclosing the two **siphons**) is so long it squirts a lot of water out when it pulls down into its burrow. Once the siphon tube is back inside the shell, the strong foot extends, expands, and pulls downward (sometimes 20 cm.). The soft-shell clam gets its name because its shell is weak and breaks easily. It is one of the most popular clams to eat.

Mystery solved!

Seaweeds

How can seaweeds have flowers
and seeds when they grow in
the water?
Hmmm...Let's look closely and
find out.

Seaweeds don't have true leaves, flowers, roots, stems, or seeds, but they do have similar structures. The main parts are leaf-like and produce food by photosynthesis. A mucus coating prevents water loss in wind and sun. Flowers aren't needed because reproductive cells are released right into nutrient-rich water. A **holdfast** structure anchors the plant like a root to rocks and sand. It doesn't need to absorb nutrients like roots would because nutrient-rich water constantly bathes the plant. Instead of a stem, a **stipe** gives a little support but allows it to float.

Seaweeds create wonderful habitats and food for many small fish and **invertebrates**. They are rich in vitamins and minerals.

Marine seaweeds belong to three main groups based on their dominant colour: red, brown, or green. Those with red-purple pigment are able to make food in the deepest water with the least light. Brown plants are usually found at medium depths. Green plants need the most light and do best in shallow water. But you will find all types washed ashore on the beach.

sea lettuce

Sea lettuce has light green tissue in thin sheets that look a lot like our salad lettuce. It is edible and used in salad and soup.

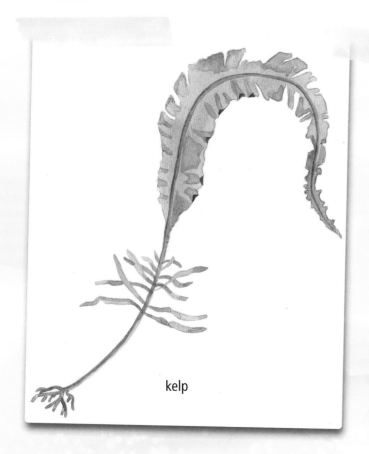

kelp

Kelp has long, brown, leathery blades that float. A **holdfast** anchors it against strong currents. It is sometimes used as fertilizer and to produce a thickener.

Irish moss is purple or purple-green and gathered on some beaches in the Maritimes. After drying and processing, a gelatin is produced and used in soup, dairy products, soap, and some cosmetics.

Irish moss

dulse

Dulse has large, rosy-purple blades. It is harvested in some places, dried, and sold in stores as a snack. Some people love it, others don't at all.

You have probably popped the bladder wrack's air bladders on the beach. These sacs keep the brown, leathery fronds afloat. The bumpy sacs at the end of the blades contain male and female cells that are released directly into water. Look for thick mats covering rocks and pilings or floating free.

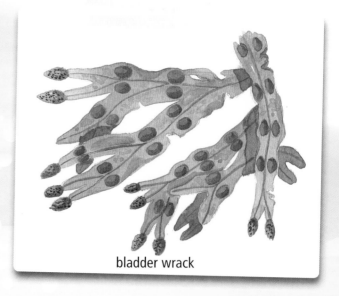
bladder wrack

Mystery solved!

Moon Snail

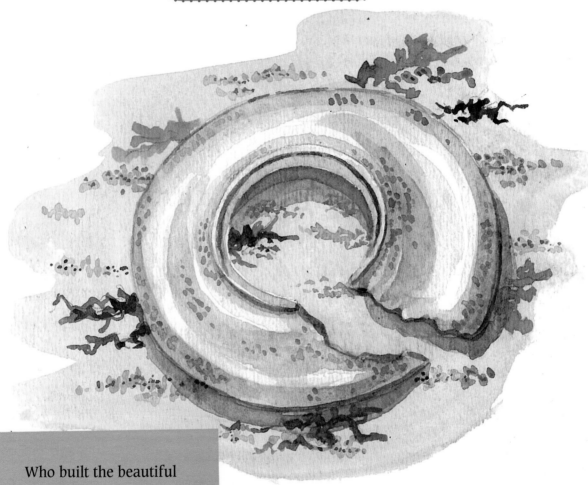

Who built the beautiful collar made of sand?

Hmmm...Let's look closely and find out.

Moon snails build these collars. When a female is ready to lay her eggs (there may be thousands), her huge slimy foot spreads sand all over her. She then cements the sand grains together with mucus. Next, eggs are laid between the sand and herself. Then a second layer of sand is formed, sandwiching the eggs. Then she leaves the wet rubbery collar. The size of the hole tells you the size of the mother. After a few weeks, the eggs hatch and break through the collar wall and it then disintegrates. Please don't damage sand collars because you will hurt the eggs inside.

A moon snail moves along the ocean floor on its huge muscular foot that constantly oozes slime. The foot can pull the snail completely under the sand, which is handy for looking for **prey**. Once the snail finds something (maybe a clam), its foot engulfs the prey. It has a toothed structure (**radula**) that drills right through a clam shell. Then a tubular mouth is inserted and sucks out the clam.

Mystery solved!

Hermit Crab

Why does a hermit crab live in a snail shell?

Hmmm...Let's look closely and find out.

All crabs have hard outer shells (called an **exoskeleton**). As it grows, the shell splits and the crab leaves. In a short while, the new larger shell hardens. However, the hermit crab has a hard shell in front but a soft, exposed abdomen in the rear. To protect itself, it finds an empty snail shell and backs into it. The hermit crab's soft abdomen is curved to fit the inside of the snail shell, and it has special short legs for anchoring itself in. Eventually it grows too large for this shell and has to find another. Sometimes there is a lot of competition for shells of the proper size. Some hermit crabs put sea anemones or sponges on their shell as camouflage.

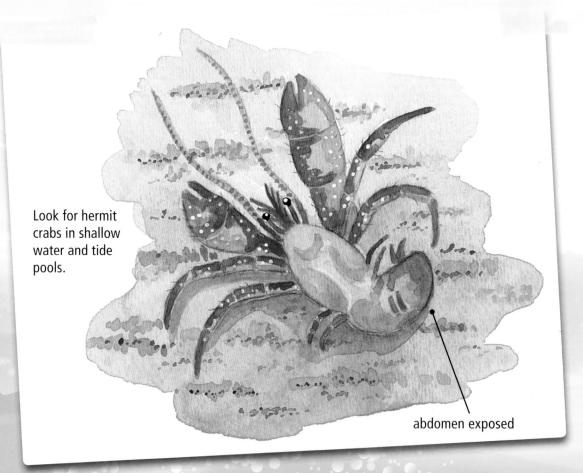

Look for hermit crabs in shallow water and tide pools.

abdomen exposed

Mystery solved!

How can a flounder blend into the ocean bottom so completely?

Hmmm…Let's look closely and find out.

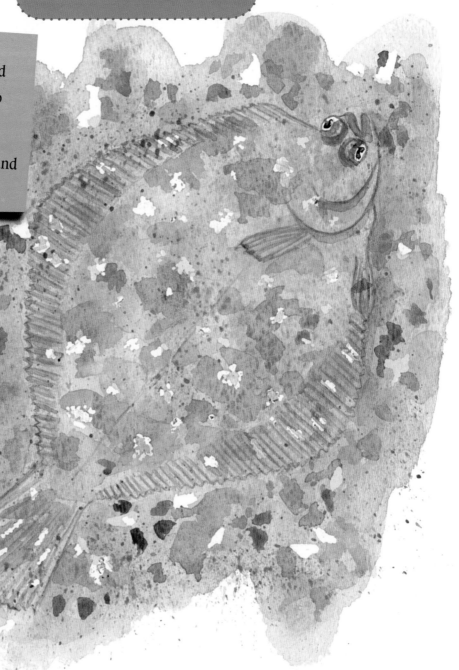

Flounder are experts at camouflage. You might not see this flat fish until you step on it in shallow water. Pigment cells on the flounder's upper surface expand and contract, creating textures and colours that copy mud, sand, pebbles, and sometimes even a checkerboard pattern. Flounder also stir up sand with their side fins and cover themselves with it. They seem to disappear from sight.

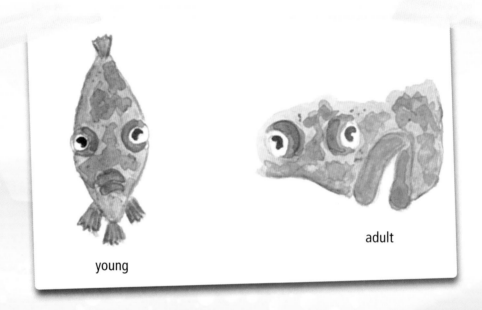

young

adult

Like other fish, a flounder starts out with an eye on each side of its body. At one month of age the left eye moves slowly to the right side and the mouth twists upward. The lower side loses pigment and becomes pale. Now the flounder can swim along the bottom finding food (crabs, sea worms, **invertebrates**) while the eyes on top watch for enemies.

Mystery solved!

Starfish

sieve plate

Can starfish re-grow from separate pieces?

Hmmm…Let's look closely and find out.

Years ago fishermen would cut starfish up into pieces and throw them back into the water because they were worried they would eat all the shellfish. However, the starfish numbers increased. This is because if a starfish arm is cut off, a new one will grow back in about a year. As long as the central disc is undamaged, some starfish recover even after losing four out of five arms.

Under the arms are hundreds of tiny tube-like feet ending in suckers. Water enters the internal system of interconnected canals through the red sieve plate on top. As muscles pump seawater in and out, the **tube feet** lengthen and contract. The suckers have amazing strength and together with muscles in the arms can pull a clam open a little. Then the starfish pushes its stomach into the shell and digests the **prey**.

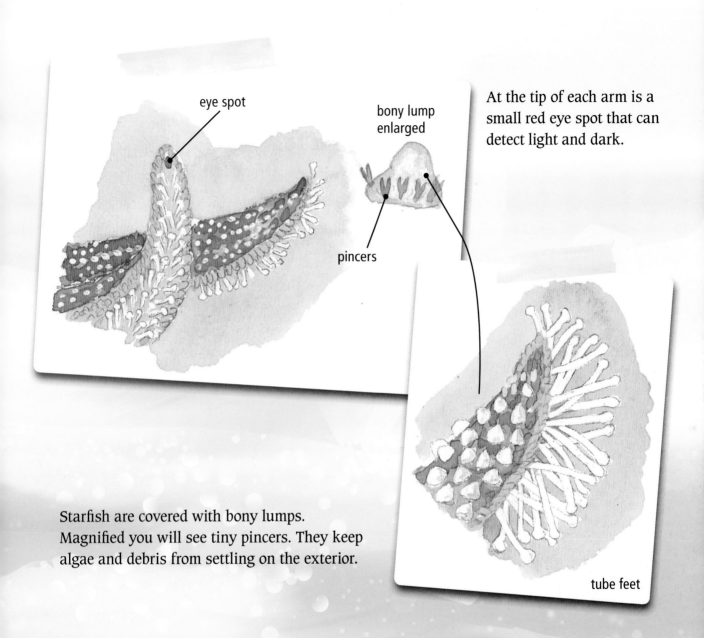

eye spot

bony lump
enlarged

At the tip of each arm is a
small red eye spot that can
detect light and dark.

pincers

tube feet

Starfish are covered with bony lumps.
Magnified you will see tiny pincers. They keep
algae and debris from settling on the exterior.

Mystery solved!

Sand Dollar

Why are some sand dollars white and others brown?

Hmmm...Let's look closely and find out.

Living sand dollars are reddish-brown. Small, short, soft spines and moveable **tube feet** cover the top and bottom. On the bottom these structures help it move through the sand, bury itself, trap microscopic food, and push the food toward a small mouth. On top is a five-pointed star with tiny holes from which tube feet stick out and are used for breathing.

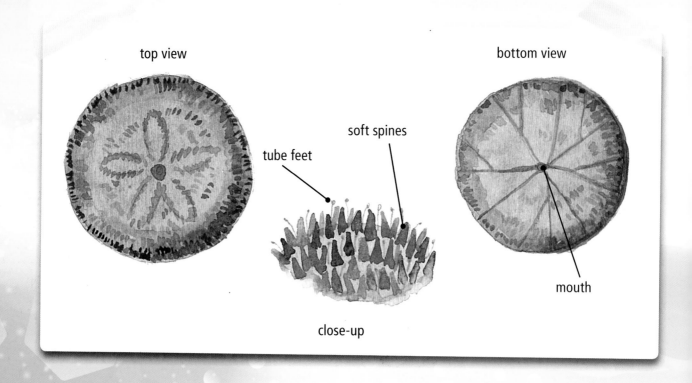

top view

bottom view

tube feet

soft spines

mouth

close-up

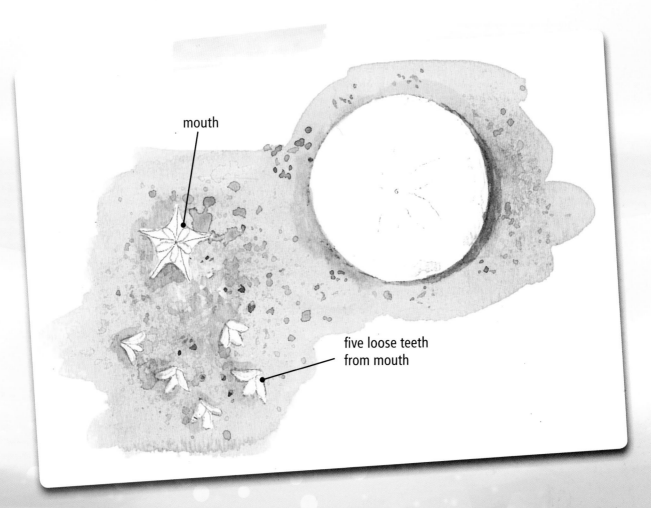

mouth

five loose teeth
from mouth

When a sand dollar dies, the spines and **tube feet** fall off and the colour fades to white. Shake one and you will hear something rattling inside. The mouth has five small teeth that open and close like a beak. At death they fall apart.

Mystery solved!

lion's mane jellyfish

jellyfish

Can dead jellyfish still sting you?

Hmmm…Let's look carefully and find out.

moon jellyfish

Jellyfish aren't fish at all but a primitive animal with jelly-like material between an inner and outer membrane. They swim along like a graceful umbrella opening and closing.

Because they aren't strong swimmers, they are at the mercy of currents and tides and often wash ashore.

Stinging cells on moon jellyfish aren't strong enough to penetrate human skin. These cells are found on the small tentacles hanging along the outside edge. However, the stinging cells on the larger lion's mane jellyfish can be very painful to people. They are located on the long stringy tentacles that hang down.

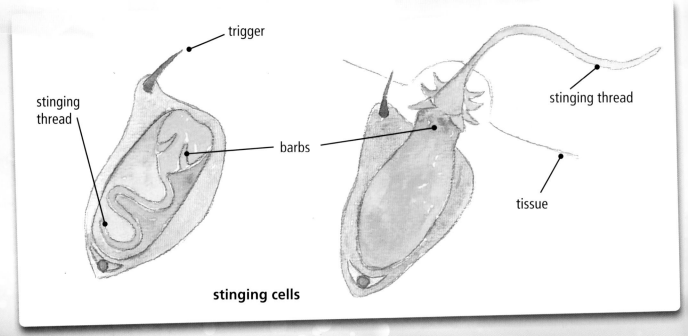

stinging cells

A trigger on each stinging cell is activated by touch or a chemical and a thread explodes out, turning inside out. This exposes barbs that hook onto tissue of a **prey**. **Toxin** is injected and usually paralyzes the tiny creature.

So if you find a lion's mane jellyfish washed up, don't touch it! Unless it has been decaying a while, **toxin** may still discharge causing stinging, cramps, itching, and even breathing difficulty.

Mystery solved!

Oysters

How do oysters form pearls?

Hmmm…Let's look closely
and find out.

Pearl oysters are different from our local oysters and live in tropical seas. When an irritating object such as sand, food, or a parasite gets stuck between the shell and **mantle** (layer of soft tissue), the oyster covers it with many layers of a pearly substance (**nacre**) to protect itself. Over time a beautiful pearl forms. Colours depend on pigment in the nacre. The shape is determined by the irritant.

Oysters found in Eastern Canada don't produce **nacre**. Because their shells are made from calcite, that is what they will cover the occasional irritant with. So the pearl formed is lustreless and of no value. However, East Coast oysters are considered a delicacy and are important to the fishing industry.

Millions of oyster eggs are released every year and hatch into free-swimming larvae. If they aren't eaten, the larvae settle on rocks, shells, and wood pilings using a cement they secrete. Mucus in the gills trap algae and other organic particles for food. Any pollutants in the water will also be concentrated in the gills, so be careful eating oysters. The purple spot inside the shell is where the oyster's muscle was attached.

Mystery solved!

Anemone

Is a sea anemone a flower or an animal?

Hmmm...Let's look closely and find out.

Although they look like beautiful flowers, sea anemone are actually animals. Our northern red sea anemone is red, sometimes with white rings. Fleshy petal-like tentacles have cells that sting **prey** (small fish, **crustaceans**, etc.) that come close and sweep them into the anemone's mouth. Once in the sea anemone's stomach, its enzymes are so strong a small crab can be digested in five minutes. The sting is not poisonous to humans.

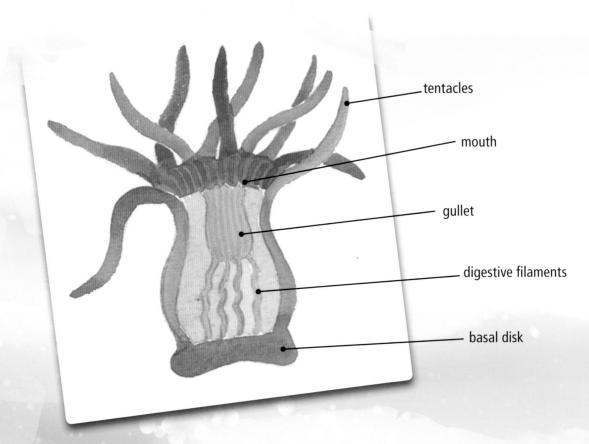

tentacles

mouth

gullet

digestive filaments

basal disk

When disturbed, tentacles are drawn inward, leaving behind a wrinkled jelly-like blob. This protects an anemone from predators or from drying out if exposed at low tide. Look for them attached to rocks, wood, sand, and seaweed. Sea anemone can move slightly from day to day on their basal disk.

Mystery solved!

Sponge

Just what is a sponge?

Hmmm...Let's look closely and find out.

deadman's finger sponge

A sponge is not a plant, but is actually an animal without a brain or central nervous system. Sponges have no mouth, stomach, or internal organs, but individual cells perform specific functions. Water enters through small pores covering the arms. Cells with tiny hair-like structures (**flagella**) beat and drive water through the central canal where plankton, organic particles, and oxygen are trapped. Water leaves through a larger pore on top. A network of tough needle-shaped fibres (spicules) give the sponge its firmness.

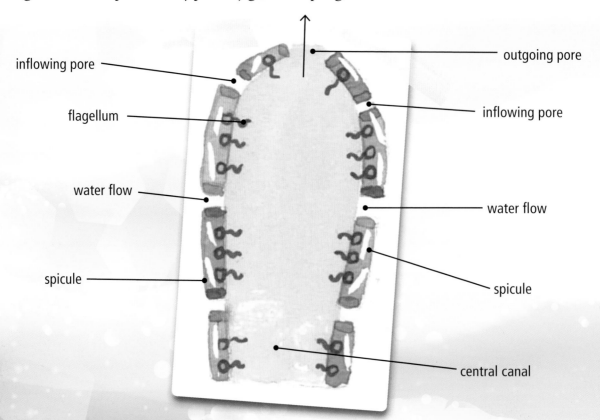

The finger sponge has a single stalk that attaches itself to rocks, shells, and pilings. As it grows, more arms are added. Pieces often break off during storms and wash onto beaches. Natural sponges bought for cleaning come from warm seas and the square, coloured ones are of course made by humans.

Mystery solved!

What can you identify?

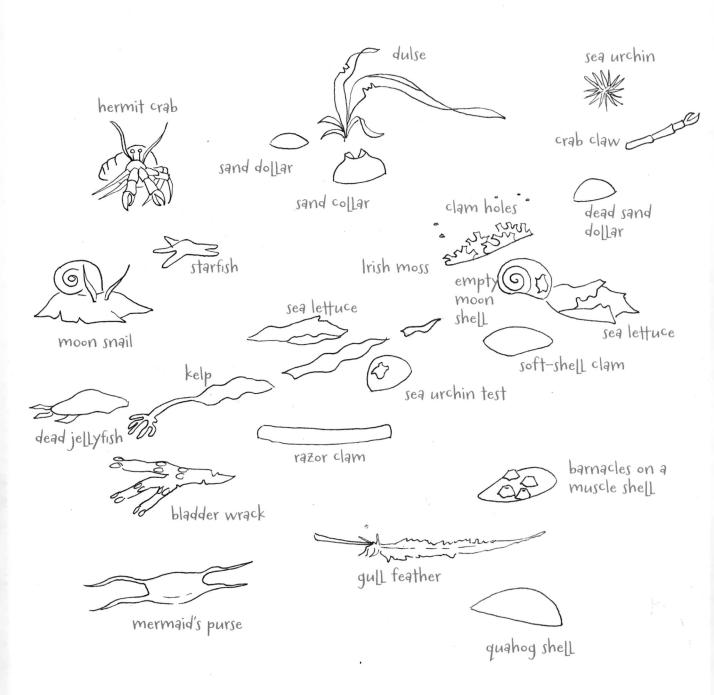

hermit crab

dulse

sea urchin

crab claw

sand dollar

sand collar

clam holes

dead sand dollar

starfish

Irish moss

empty moon shell

moon snail

sea lettuce

sea lettuce

soft-shell clam

kelp

sea urchin test

dead jellyfish

razor clam

barnacles on a muscle shell

bladder wrack

gull feather

mermaid's purse

quahog shell

Glossary

crustacean: Animals with a segmented body, hard outer skeleton, paired jointed limbs. Includes barnacles, lobsters, crabs.

exoskeleton: A hard outer structure that provides protection and support.

flagellum: Small hair-like structures.

holdfast: A stucture that fastens something securely.

invertebrate: An animal that lacks a backbone.

mantle: Soft tissue layer covering the body of oysters and other mollusks that secrets a substance that forms a shell.

mollusk: A group of animals that have soft bodies and usually a shell (snails, oysters, clams).

nacre: A shiny compound produced by some mollusks that forms an inner shell and also the coating of pearls.

prey: An animal that is killed for food.

radula: A structure with tiny teeth that is used for scraping food.

siphon: Tubes that are used to transport fluid.

stipe: A stalk or stem.

toxin: A poisonous substance.

tube feet: Small muscular tubes that are used for food handling, movement, breathing, and anchoring.

References

Fardon, John. *Oceans, The Ultimate Guide to Marine Life*. San Diego, CA: Miles Kelly, 2011.

Gibson, Merritt. *Seashores of the Maritimes*. Halifax, NS: Nimbus, 2003.

Gosner, Kenneth L. *A Field Guide to the Atlantic Seashore*. Boston: Houghton Mifflin, 1978.

Hickman, Pamela. *At the Seashore*. Halifax, NS: Formac, 1996.

Kochanoff, Peggy. *Beachcombing the Atlantic Coast*. Missoula, MT. Mountain Press, 1997.

Lawlor, Elizabeth P. *Discover Nature at the Seashore*. Harrisburg, PA: Stackpole Books, 1992.

Parker, Steve. *Seashore Eyewitness Book*. New York, NY: Alfred A. Knopf, 1989.

Zim, Herbert S. and Ingle, Lester. *Seashores, A Golden Nature Guide*. New York: Simon and Schuster, 1955.

Web Sites

Canadian Wildlife Federation: www.cwf-fcf.org

National Geographic for Kids: www.kids.nationalgeographic.com

National Wildlife Federation: www.nwf.org

Ranger Rick's Green Zone: www.nwf.org/rrgreenzone

Robert Bateman's "Get to Know" Program: www.get-to-know.org